QUEEN ELIZABETH I

A Life From Beginning to End

Table of Contents

Introduction

From the moment she was conceived, Queen Elizabeth I of England was the subject of controversy. The daughter of King Henry VIII and his second wife Anne Boleyn, Elizabeth was accused of being illegitimate by English Catholics before she was even born, as they refused to acknowledge the annulment of Henry's first marriage. Elizabeth's childhood was tumultuous, as her mother was executed when she was two and a half years old, and she was raised as Henry's daughter but not Henry's heir.

Elizabeth became Queen in 1558, succeeding her half-sister Mary Tudor to the throne. Elizabeth refused to marry immediately and rule as co-regent with her husband, as Mary had done, and her decision to remain single and rule alone became a defining feature of her reign. However, Elizabeth knew that by entertaining the notion of marriage to a foreign prince she could maintain control of her own political authority. Naming an heir, whether from her own body of not, would destabilize her position and leave her vulnerable to a coup.

Elizabeth's voluntary decision to never marry inspired a cult of virginity where the Queen's decision to remain a virgin gradually became regarded as her greatest virtue. Poets, writers, and artists fueled the public's worship of her virtue by creating recognizable iconography that created a legend around Elizabeth, even while she was still alive. Elizabeth's loyal subjects often pointed out that her reign fulfilled one of the prophecies of Merlin, "then shall a Royal Virgin reign, which shall stretch her white rod over the Belgic shore and the great Castile smite so sore withal that it shall make him shake and fall." The "great Castile," of course, referred to King Philip of Spain.

When Elizabeth succeeded to the throne of England, the country was divided along religious lines. A Protestant Queen, Elizabeth was relatively tolerant of Catholics in England and managed to avoid widespread persecution; while Mary Tudor will be forever remembered as "Bloody Mary" for her bloodthirsty persecution of English Protestants, Elizabeth is lauded for her even-handed approach. One of her mottoes, "video et taceo" (I see but say nothing), reflects this. Not everything Elizabeth is remembered for is positive, though; in the later years of her reign Elizabeth had her cousin Mary Queen of Scots executed, and a series of economic and military problems weakened her popularity.

A Queen for forty-five years, Elizabeth's reign became known as the Elizabethan era, a golden age of exploration, triumph over foreign aggressors, and relative domestic peace that prompted the beginnings of the English Renaissance.

Chapter One

Early Years

"Two beheadings out of six wives is too many."

—King Henry VIII of England

Elizabeth Tudor was born on the 7th of September 1533 at the Palace of Placentia in Greenwich, England, the first and only daughter of King Henry VIII of England and his second wife, Anne Boleyn. Elizabeth's birth was significant as just four months earlier Katherine of Aragon, Henry VIII's first wife, had been formally stripped of her title as queen and Anne Boleyn had been crowned Queen Consort of England. Anne was incredibly unpopular with the English people, and her position was precarious as Henry VIII was desperate for a son and male heir to continue the Tudor line after his death. Having divorced one wife, Henry had nothing stopping him from doing it again. That Elizabeth was a girl was a disappointment to both of her parents; a traditional jousting tournament planned to celebrate the arrival of a male heir, was canceled.

Elizabeth was given a magnificent christening, and for the first two years and eight months of her life, she lived in absolute luxury, with her own household and staff of over 250 servants to tend to her every need. On her birth,

Elizabeth became the heir presumptive to the throne of England, but she was not Henry VIII's first child born into wedlock - and therefore not his first heir. Katherine of Aragon had also given Henry a daughter, Mary, who lost her position as heir when Henry annulled his marriage to her mother. With Anne's encouragement, Henry separated Mary from her own household of servants, forcing her to live with Elizabeth at Hatfield House under dramatically reduced circumstances. Labeled a bastard, Mary was rejected by her father, separated from her mother, and endured many difficult years of solitude.

Two years and eight months after Elizabeth's birth, Anne Boleyn was charged with adultery, incest, and high treason. That Anne was actually guilty of these crimes is unlikely, and the charges are thought to have been fabricated by her enemy, Henry's chief advisor Thomas Cromwell, to get her out of the way. Henry's interest in Anne had waned as she experienced a number of unsuccessful pregnancies after giving birth to Elizabeth, and her behavior was said to be too immodest and tempestuous to last as Queen Consort of England. Guilty or not, Anne was beheaded on the 19th of May 1536; Elizabeth was declared illegitimate and formally removed from the line of succession.

Henry VIII remarried and his new wife, Jane Seymour, quickly gave him a son, whom the couple named Edward. Elizabeth was moved into Edward's household where she was no longer the principal heir but did receive a first-class education. Elizabeth learned Flemish, Italian, Spanish, French and Greek, languages she grew so proficient in that as an adult she could speak each as well as her native tongue. Elizabeth was praised as a brilliant scholar with an acute mind and formidable memory from a young age, and she readily absorbed the ideals of the "reformed faith" followers, or Protestants, she was surrounded by.

On Henry's death in 1547 Edward, now nine years old, became King Edward VI, and Elizabeth joined Catherine Parr, Henry's sixth wife and widow, at her household in Chelsea. Catherine was married surprisingly soon after Henry's death to Admiral Thomas Seymour, an uncle to Edward. At Chelsea, Elizabeth's formal education continued, but she soon became prey to inappropriate behavior from Thomas Seymour. When Thomas' penchant for tickling and slapping the young Elizabeth in her nightgown developed into further indecency, Catherine stepped in; in May 1548 Elizabeth was sent back to Hatfield House. Catherine died in childbirth, and when the King's council heard of Thomas's behavior with Elizabeth, second in line to the throne of England, he was arrested on suspicion of plotting to marry her. The fact that he was found outside the bedroom of the young King Edward with a loaded pistol did not help his cause, and he was later executed.

King Edward VI died of tuberculosis in 1553, aged just fifteen. Mary, the daughter of Katherine of Aragon, was next in line to the throne according to the last Act of Succession passed by Henry VIII. However, on Edward's death John Dudley, Duke of Northumberland, staged a coup and tried to put Protestant Lady Jean Grey on the throne in place of Catholic Mary. The English people rose up to thwart the coup and those behind it were executed, including the unfortunate Lady Jean Grey.

Queen Mary Tudor was the first female monarch of England and ruled for five difficult and unhappy years. Desperate to produce a male heir to whom she could pass her throne, and keen to forge an alliance with other Catholic powers in Europe, Mary agreed to marry the premier Catholic leader in Europe, Philip of Spain. This marriage was ill-judged, and Mary instantly lost the support of the English people, who saw Mary and Philip's joint rule as England's submission to the Kingdom of Spain. For Philip, the marriage was purely political, and when Mary became ill, after two phantom pregnancies that may have actually been symptoms of ovarian or stomach cancer, Philip deserted her, and Mary died alone.

During her short reign, Mary had introduced laws of heresy that sanctioned the burning of over 300 Protestants at the stake, which earned her the sobriquet "Bloody Mary," but she had failed to properly re-establish the Holy Roman Empire's dominance in England. What's more, in the final year of Mary's reign, England lost Calais to the French, the last symbolic remnant of a medieval English empire. The French King, Henry II, was also enjoying a military presence in Scotland and the support of King James V. England's power in Europe was negligible against the power of the European Counter-Reformation that had the support of the Papacy; to make matters worse, her treasury was empty. This was the England that Elizabeth inherited when, on the 17th of November 1558, aged just twenty-five, she ascended to the throne of England.

Chapter Two

Becoming Queen of England

"And as I am but one body naturally considered, though by His permission a body politic to govern, so shall I desire you all ... to be assistant to me, that I with my ruling and you with your service may make a good account to Almighty God and leave some comfort to our posterity on earth. I mean to direct all my actions by good advice and counsel."

—Queen Elizabeth I of England

On the afternoon of the day of her accession, Elizabeth summoned the council to Hatfield House to discuss her immediate plans. If any of Elizabeth's council had been concerned about the young Queen's lack of political experience or religious stance they were immediately put at ease by Elizabeth's self-possessed manner. Among the men at this meeting was William Cecil, a man who had prospered while King Edward VI was on the throne and had worked his way through prestigious positions at court, eventually being knighted in 1551. Cecil's career stagnated during Mary's rule as he shared Elizabeth's dedication to Protestantism, but Elizabeth recognized Cecil's expertise on financial matters and fervent patriotism right away - Cecil soon became Elizabeth's closest advisor. Before long Elizabeth came to refer to

Cecil as her "spirit" and to respect his advice and counsel over all others.

At this meeting, Elizabeth also appointed Lord Robert Dudley as Master of the Horse. Dudley's appointment was controversial as he was the son of the Duke of Northumberland, the powerful noble at the center of the Lady Jean Grey plot to oust both Mary and Elizabeth from the line of succession. Elizabeth had known Dudley since they were children and he was greatly skilled in equine matters, so she was willing to overlook his part in the treason, a decision some of her advisors saw as evidence of her poor judgment.

From her first official day as Queen, Elizabeth busied herself appointing councilors, drafting policies, and organizing her household. Meanwhile in France King Henry II publicly declared that as a bastard Elizabeth was unfit to rule and that the true Queen of England was his own niece, Mary Queen of Scots. Many English Catholics who had staunchly refused to acknowledge King Henry VIII's divorce from Katherine of Aragon shared Henry II's view. This pressure pushed Elizabeth into an early alliance with King Philip of Spain, Queen Mary Tudor's widowed husband, who had already expressed a wish to marry her. Elizabeth had no intention of marrying Philip but knew that an alliance with Spain was crucial to ensure that Henry II and his Catholic supporters did not enlist the help of the Pope to deny her legitimacy as Queen. What's more, Elizabeth hoped that Philip would help her to win Calais back from the French.

The whole of London came out to see their new Queen make her historic procession into the city. After lodging for one week in the Tower of London, the very place Elizabeth had been held as a prisoner in fear of execution by Mary, she moved into Whitehall Palace. Elizabeth was dignified and artful in her manner during these public appearances, making a point of greeting the most common people who in turn fell in love with her youth and majesty. Throughout December and early January, preparations were being made for Elizabeth's coronation, a celebration intended to be as spectacular and extravagant as anything King Henry VIII pulled off during his reign.

On the 12th of January 1559, Elizabeth boarded her barge and traveled up the Thames River to the Tower. The next day, dressed in a lavish gown made of twenty-three yards of cloth of gold, trimmed with ermine and layered with gold lace, Elizabeth headed a procession of over a thousand mounted dignitaries and was carried in state through four miles of London streets. The Queen presided over a number of magnificent pageants, most of which explicitly promoted Protestantism, and gave a number of speeches, which were received with pleasure by her rejoicing subjects. On Sunday the 15th of January 1559, Elizabeth led another procession from Westminster Hall to Westminster Abbey where she was finally crowned Queen. Elizabeth's coronation ceremony is notable, not only for its richness and extravagance but for being the last in England conducted according to Medieval Latin rubric. Elizabeth was anointed by the Catholic Bishop

Oglethorpe of Carlisle, and when she was finally presented for the people's acceptance, the Abbey erupted with shouts of joy and loud crashing trumpets, organs, and bells.

Chapter Three

The Matter of Succession

"In the end, this shall be for me sufficient, that a marble stone shall declare that a queen, having reigned such a time, lived and died a virgin."

—Queen Elizabeth I of England

Elizabeth opened her first Parliament on the 25th of January 1559 wearing her coronation robes. Forty-six peers were in attendance, and Elizabeth took this opportunity to make it absolutely clear that she intended to be an engaged and active sovereign and would not take kindly to any attempt by Commons members to manipulate her. The first and perhaps most pressing matter of Elizabeth's early reign was her marital status. Days after Parliament opened, Commons drew up a formal petition asking the Queen to marry as soon as possible to safeguard against any threats to her succession. The Queen was taken aback by the boldness of this request and responded with a statement she was to repeat time and time again during her reign, "I am already bound unto a husband, which is the kingdom of England." Elizabeth assured her peers that the matter of succession would be taken care of but that she intended to leave the identity of her successor for divine providence to decide.

There are a number of possible reasons for Elizabeth's disinclination towards marriage. Having been heir to the English throne from the moment of her birth, Elizabeth had experienced first-hand the constant simmering threat of rebellion. Elizabeth had also expressed fear that any male heir she produced might turn on her and attempt to overthrow her himself. Parliament was unnerved by Elizabeth's speech, which ended with the words, "In the end, this shall be for me sufficient, that a marble stone shall declare that a queen, having reigned such a time, lived and died a virgin."

It has been speculated since that Elizabeth's wish to remain a virgin was the result of trauma. Elizabeth was around eight years old when her father's teenaged wife, Katherine Howard, was executed for adultery, just as her mother had been, and watched as Thomas Seymour, the man with whom she had her first sexual experiences, was put to death. It is possible that in Elizabeth's mind sex was always inextricably linked with death. It has also been suggested that Elizabeth somehow knew herself to be infertile and knew that refusing to marry was the only way for her to retain agency over her body.

Yet Elizabeth never ruled marriage out completely and used the lure of her single status to manipulate foreign powers who hoped to share her kingdom and influence England's role overseas by securing a political match. De Feria, King Philip of Spain's ambassador in England, presented Elizabeth with a marriage proposal from Philip in February 1559. Elizabeth expressed the many virtues of living her life as a virgin, to which De Feria responded that if she failed to marry and produce an heir the King of France would put Mary Queen of Scots on her throne instead. Furious at this suggestion, Elizabeth was nonetheless aware that England needed the friendship of Spain to deter France from acts of aggression and did not turn him down directly but took time to deliberate.

The matter was put to members of Parliament, who were aghast that Elizabeth would even consider Philip's proposal. Not only was Philip far too close to Elizabeth in affinity, being the widow of her half-sister, but Philip's position as premier leader of the Catholic Church was completely at odds with Parliament's hopes of re-establishing Protestantism in England. Elizabeth waited until a religious settlement and peace treaty with France was all but finalized before formally rejecting Philip's proposal and at the same time asserted her religious stance, stating that "she could not marry your Majesty because she is a heretic." In early April a peace treaty was secured between England and France and France and Spain known as the Treaty of Cateau-Cambresis. The treaty stipulated that Calais should remain the property of France for eight years; once it was signed, Philip immediately married Elizabeth of Valois.

With a peace treaty now in place and Philip's proposal successfully declined, Elizabeth turned her attention to religious reform. Elizabeth's very legitimacy as Queen was rejected by many Catholics who never acknowledged Henry VIII's annulment of his marriage to Katharine of

Aragon, and many in Parliament feared that there would be an uprising during the early days of Elizabeth's reign. This fear that grew in intensity when, in February 1599, the Pope issued a Bull declaring that all rulers who supported heretical doctrines should be deposed by the faithful. It was a none-too-subtle threat to Elizabeth, one she sought to minimize by treading a middle path between Catholics and radical Puritans.

Elizabeth abhorred fanaticism and tried to avoid offending Catholic neighbors in Europe while asserting the rights of her Protestant subjects. Elizabeth insisted that public worship be conducted in English, but much to the horror of her stricter Protestant subjects, she insisted on retaining certain Catholic rituals. According to the Queen, Holy Communion could be performed but only according to the Book of Common Prayer. Heresy laws were repealed, and attendance to church on Sunday became mandatory. On the 19th of April 1559, Parliament put forth the Acts of Supremacy and Uniformity that made Protestantism the official religion of England and made Elizabeth the Supreme Governor of the Church of England. Matthew Parker, once the chaplain of Anne Boleyn, was enlisted as Elizabeth's Archbishop of Canterbury.

Chapter Four

The Edinburgh Treaty

"I would rather go to any extreme than suffer anything that is unworthy of my reputation, or of that of my crown."

—Queen Elizabeth I

A number of willing candidates were paraded before Elizabeth during her first years as Queen in the hope that she would select one of them to be her King. After denying Philip of Spain her hand in marriage, Elizabeth entertained the idea of marrying Charles, Archduke of Austria and member of the powerful Hapsburg family, and briefly considered Prince Erik of Sweden as a suitor. Closer to home, two men of noble blood, Henry FitzAlan and Sir William Pickering vied for Elizabeth's attention. Elizabeth enjoyed the attention these young men gave her and was shrewd enough to use the influence she had over foreign princes to her advantage, but she played her cards close to her chest. Only one man was a serious contender for the Queen's affections at this time, and his name was Robert Dudley.

Robert Dudley was a childhood friend of Elizabeth's and, at the time of her accession, he was married to Amy Robsart. Amy was ill, mostly likely suffering from breast cancer, and many speculated that when Amy passed away,

Elizabeth would marry Dudley. While naysayers criticized Dudley as a self-serving man who fabricated his feelings for the Queen to further his ambitions, there is now little doubt that the love between Elizabeth and Dudley was real and mutual. As Elizabeth's preferential treatment of Dudley grew more intense, so too did the scandal surrounding them.

Around the same time that Elizabeth formally turned down Austrian Archduke Charles II's proposal of marriage, she made Dudley a Knight of the Garter and later raised him to Lord Lieutenant and Constable of Windsor Castle. William Cecil, Elizabeth's most trusted advisor, and a number of other conservative peers made their disapproval of the relationship clear, and there were murmurings of rebellion amongst the nobility. As ill-feeling between pro- and anti-Dudley factions at court intensified there were even plots to assassinate him. Acting to protect the throne of England and secure his own position, Cecil made every attempt to put a marriage between Elizabeth and Archduke Charles back on the table, but the Queen would not be pressured and continued to draw out negotiations for a number of months, at times intimating that she was seriously considering the marriage only to express her desire to become a nun the next day.

England came under serious threat from Scotland and France in 1560 when Elizabeth sent English troops to support the Protestant Lords of Scotland. Mary of Guise - the widow of King James V of Scotland, mother of Mary Queen of Scots and a powerful figure in France - was determined to bring French troops to Scotland to support her daughter's legitimacy as Queen of England. Elizabeth blocked Mary Guise's army from landing, leading to a battle between the English and Scottish at Leith, during which many lost their lives. In June 1560, Mary of Guise died of dropsy, opening the way for a peace treaty between England, Scotland, and France. William Cecil was dispatched to Scotland immediately, where he secured the signing of the Edinburgh Treaty. The treaty stipulated that Mary Queen of Scots would desist from claiming the throne of England to be hers; in turn, the English and French would not interfere with politics in the kingdom of Scotland.

In September 1560, Dudley's wife Amy died under suspicious circumstances as the result of a fall down a staircase. Elizabeth distanced herself from the tragedy by insisting that Dudley leave court while a full investigation was carried out, and Cecil was immediately brought back into her favor and confidence. The coroner held Dudley's life in the palm of his hand as they deliberated over the cause of Amy's death. Eventually, the jury concluded that there could be no "presumption of evil," the verdict was accidental death, and Dudley was acquitted from any responsibility. Despite this, few believed in Dudley's innocence and even went as far as to suggest that Elizabeth had colluded in Amy's murder.

Elizabeth needed Dudley and the world to know that she was still in control of her own destiny and made it clear that she would never marry Robert Dudley, a mere subject. Following months of badgering from Dudley to raise him to the peerage, Elizabeth relented and organized the relevant ceremony. There, in front of astounded courtiers, Elizabeth took a knife and cut up the Letters Patent, stating that she would not have "another Dudley in the House of Lords as his family had been traitors for three generations." Dudley was humiliated, but gradually the crisis passed, the gossip died down, and Dudley returned to his position as the Queen's favorite courtier.

Chapter Five

Mary Queen of Scots

"In my end is my beginning."

—Mary Queen of Scots

Mary Stuart was born in 1542 and succeeded her father, James V, to the throne of Scotland within a week of her birth. As a child, she was sent to France to be raised at the court of Henry II and was betrothed to the Dauphin Francis, whom she married when she was fifteen years old. The Dauphin Francis became King in 1559 and Mary became Queen Consort of France. In England, Henry VIII's last will and testament had excluded the Stuarts from succeeding to the English throne, yet when Elizabeth became Queen, many contested her right and claimed that she was illegitimate. As the senior descendant of Henry VIII's elder sister Margaret, Mary Stuart, they said, was the rightful Queen of England.

The relationship between Elizabeth and Mary was politically and emotionally complex. Mary had refused to ratify the Treaty of Edinburgh of 1560 and denied even being Elizabeth's heir, regarding herself as the indisputable rightful Queen of England. Some historians have suggested that Elizabeth was jealous of her taller, more attractive, and younger cousin, who had been raised at the French court and was far worldlier than she. King Francis' death in 1560 also made Mary an incredibly desirable young widow, making Elizabeth only the second-most attractive marriage prospect for European princes and kings. On the other hand, Elizabeth clearly felt an affinity with her cousin, who was both a blood relative and a fellow female sovereign ruling alone over her kingdom.

Elizabeth expressed a desire to meet with Mary in person to go over the wording of the Treaty of Edinburgh and come to an agreement that suited them both. Mary sent an ambassador with warm greetings to begin the process and made it clear that were she to denounce her claim to the throne she would expect to be publicly named as Elizabeth's successor. Elizabeth could not agree to these terms as, as she put it, "more people worship the rising than the setting sun" and to name her successor would seriously undermine her own authority and the security of her place on the throne.

After months of frustrated negotiations, preparations eventually got underway for a meeting between Elizabeth and Mary in York, scheduled sometime between August 20th and September 20th, 1562. Right then a religious war between Catholics and Protestant Huguenots broke out in France. Elizabeth could defy her advisors no longer and was forced to cancel the meeting with Mary, who was supporting the Catholic cause, in order to intervene in France.

Before Elizabeth could dispatch six thousand Englishmen to assist the Huguenots in France, she became gravely ill with smallpox. The Queen came so close to death that the distraught Privy Council was forced to convene to discuss the urgent matter of succession. On what many believed to be her deathbed, Elizabeth expressed her wish that Lord Dudley be appointed Lord Protector until the issue of succession was resolved. This would never be agreed to and, to some, offered further evidence that Elizabeth had still intended to marry Dudley.

Thankfully, Elizabeth recovered, but Parliament decided that they had let the matter of the Queen's marriage lie for too long and began pressuring her to marry and supply England with an heir. Queen Mary's own marriage plans added fuel to the fire as she declared her interest in marrying Don Carlos of Spain, a clear enemy of England. Elizabeth found herself in an impossible situation, forced to name an heir knowing that that heir would then become the focus of uprisings against her. The closest in line to Elizabeth's throne was Lady Katherine Grey, the older sister of Lady Jean Grey. Katherine had married the Earl of Hertford without Elizabeth's consent; an act of treason, considering any children she had would be in the line of succession. When Elizabeth found out that Katherine was with child, she locked Katherine and Hertford up in the Tower of London. The couple had two sons while incarcerated and remained in the Tower until Katherine's death from tuberculosis in 1568, at which point Cecil took Katherine's sons into his own home and raised them as his own.

To dissuade Mary from marrying into the Spanish royal family, Elizabeth devised a plan for her to marry her own closest friend, Lord Dudley. To make Dudley more desirable to Mary, Elizabeth created him Baron Denbigh and Earl of Leicester but to no avail, Mary had absolutely no interest in marrying Lord Leicester, and he had no interest in marrying her. Mary turned her attention to Lord Darnley, son of the House of Lennox, who carried his own claim to the English throne, but it was highly unlikely that Elizabeth would agree to the match.

Letters continued to bounce back and forth between the two Queens with neither giving in to the other's demands until, on the 29th of July, 1565, Mary Queen of Scots married Lord Darnley in a lavish Catholic ceremony at Holyrood Palace. Whether Elizabeth had allowed Darnley to go to Mary in Scotland out of blind faith or whether she engineered the whole affair, knowing that Darnley would lead to Mary's downfall, is hard to discern. Mary had slighted Elizabeth by marrying one of her subjects with no discussion, but her actions hurt her more than Elizabeth, as her marriage to Darnley quickly turned sour. Darnley was an insolent, haughty man and was frequently drunk and violent. Jealous of Mary's close relationship with her secretary Rizzio, Darnley stood by as a group of disgruntled rebels murdered Rizzio as he dined with Mary at Holyrood Palace. Mary was six months pregnant at the time.

On the 19th of June Mary gave birth to a healthy son, James, in the safety of the fortified sanctuary at Edinburgh Castle. Elizabeth was named godmother. When Mary wrote to Elizabeth describing the horrors she had endured and Darnley's involvement Elizabeth was aghast. By now Mary was desperate to be officially separated from Darnley, but there was no chance of an annulment. Mary turned to James Hepburn, Earl of Bothwell, who happily slid into the void that had been created with Darnley's absence. In February 1567, Darnley was murdered in an attack almost certainly headed by Bothwell. Whether Mary knew about the planned assassination or not is unclear, but Mary's decision to marry Bothwell mere weeks after Darnley's murder put her under great suspicion.

The Scots lords were disgusted by the match and the Scots people turned against Mary, degrading her as she rode through the streets of Edinburgh with placards depicting her as a mermaid, a 16th-century symbol for a prostitute. Mary was imprisoned in Loch Leven Castle, and her son James was taken from her. The Scots Lords forced Mary to abdicate in favor of her infant son, who was taken to Stirling Castle to be raised as a Protestant while the lords ruled as regents. Elizabeth found the Scots' treatment of their Queen deplorable and was determined to secure Mary's release, even threatening to wage war on the Scots. To complicate matters Mary escaped Loch Leven Castle on the 2nd of May and, her supporters defeated on the battlefield at Langside, she rode to England where she was sure her cousin and fellow Queen would help her.

Chapter Six

The Casket Letters and Ridolfi Plot

"The Queen of Scots is, and always shall be, a dangerous person to your estate."

—Sir William Cecil

During Mary's long and dangerous ride south she shaved her head to avoid being recognized and subsisted on porridge and milk. When Mary finally arrived in Carlisle English authorities were unsure of how to treat her and so kept her under guard. The conundrum of what exactly they should do with their uninvited guest would be debated back and forth between Elizabeth and her government for the next nineteen years.

At first, Elizabeth was adamant that Mary be restored at once with English help, but Cecil disagreed and reminded Elizabeth that Mary was her enemy and had been plotting to take her throne for years. If Elizabeth sent Mary back to Scotland, she would certainly be killed. If Elizabeth allowed Mary to remain in England, she would inspire every Catholic in the land to turn against her. If Elizabeth helped Mary to escape abroad she would be responsible for starting a war with Scotland, and if

King Philip diverted his epic army to help Mary take back her Scottish throne - and the English throne for the bargain - Elizabeth would be ruined.

It was decided that Mary would stay in custody but with the status of guest, not a prisoner, a distinction that came to mean very little as Elizabeth began to belittle Mary purposefully. Before Elizabeth would agree to receive Mary at court and open up negotiations for restoring her to her throne she had to have proof that Mary was innocent in the murder of Darnley, her husband. Elizabeth set up a tribunal on which six earls acted as commissioners; Elizabeth herself acted as judge to decide Mary's fate.

The inquiry began on the 4th of October in York. Moray, Mary's half-brother and the man responsible for leading the rebellion against her, appeared at the inquiry where he produced the infamous Casket Letters. This box of nine letters supposedly offers solid evidence that Mary and Bothwell plotted together to kill Darnley, but were they forgeries? We can never know for sure, as the Casket Letters no longer exist, but the English commissioners and Council saw them as enough proof that Mary was guilty. However, as Elizabeth refused to allow Mary to attend the proceedings and speak in her own defense, a guilty verdict could not be declared. This was the catch-22 situation Mary found herself caught in for the next two decades, not declared innocent but not declared guilty.

The Duke of Norfolk hatched a plan to marry Mary and bag the crowns of England and Scotland for himself. While court buzzed with gossip of Norfolk's plan,

Catholics in England rose up to defend the woman they believed to be their true Queen under the leadership of Northern Catholic lords, Northumberland and Derby. Mary had already made contact with Spain, whose relationship with England had been deteriorating, and promised that should they help her to escape she would become Queen of England in three months. The Spanish ambassador had been instrumental in initiating this rebellion, and now over 2500 men marched south, ransacking Durham Cathedral and advancing on Tutbury, where Mary was being held. The rebellion was quashed, and in all, 750 men were executed on Elizabeth's orders. Another rebellion followed, led by Lord Dacre, but this too was brutally quashed by English troops.

Hearing news of the rebellions and believing them to have been successful, the Pope Pius V further intensified the push to free Mary by issuing a bull on the 25th of February 1570 excommunicating Elizabeth and releasing her subjects from any allegiance to her. The bull, titled Regnans in Excelsis, gave a huge boost to the English Catholic cause and threatened any Catholic who obeyed Elizabeth's orders with excommunication. In turn, English Protestants hardened their resolve to protect their Queen and their faith and pressed for harsher punishments for anyone practicing Catholicism in England. Elizabeth could do little to stop England's religious problem becoming a dangerously political one; however, she did use her authority to stop the harshest legislative initiatives suggested by Parliament becoming law.

In January 1571, Roberto Ridolfi, a Florentine and papal agent, reached out to Mary and offered to act as her representative in Europe to stir up support for her cause. It was as though Mary's prayers had been answered as Ridolfi promised to secure enough Catholic support to invade England, overthrow Elizabeth, and put Mary and Norfolk in her place. Mary embroiled Norfolk in the plan and sent Ridolfi to Rome where the Pope happily blessed his plan. The Duke was then received by King Philip II who finalized plans for the Duke of Alva to invade England with 6000 Spanish troops, but news of the conspiracy leaked before it could be carried out and was abandoned. Elizabeth's attitude to Mary hardened dramatically after the Ridolfi plot, and she gave up any pretense of hoping to restore her to her throne.

Negotiations to form a union with the Austrian Archduke Charles were again opened up, and a new marriage proposal arrived from Charles IX of France's brother and heir, Henry, Duke of Anjou. This union promised a long period of political stability between England and France and would minimize the threat from Spain, but the pair were disastrously ill-matched - by now Elizabeth was 34 and the Duke just 19 - and the proposal was eventually turned down.

Chapter Seven

The Last Suitor

"A strength to harm is perilous in the hand of an ambitious head."

—Queen Elizabeth I of England

Elizabeth believed that, as sovereign, she possessed absolute power over her subjects and by extension Parliament, which was composed of them. As a result, Elizabeth often clashed with Parliament and managed to call it just ten times across the entirety of her forty-four-year reign. One such meeting of Parliament took place on 8th of May 1572 for the purpose of airing an extensive list of all of Mary Queen of Scots' misdeeds and demanding that she be put to death. Parliament was unanimously in favor of executing Mary, and Elizabeth alone insisted that Mary was a foreign prince and as such could not be put to death under English law. Parliament conceded but insisted that a bill be passed making Mary's claim to the throne void and the mention of its existence a punishable offense. Having spared Mary's life, for now, Elizabeth was forced to give up on her delaying tactics and sign a warrant for Norfolk's execution.

In April 1572, England and France concluded the Treaty of Blois, an agreement that united the two countries against Catholic Spain and the Protestant states of the Netherlands. However, in August of the same year Elizabeth was horrified to learn of the Massacre of St. Bartholomew. It began with an unpopular wedding between King Charles IX's sister Marguerite de Valois and the Protestant King Henry of Navarre. The powerful and Catholic House of Guise rebelled against the match and tried to murder a high-ranking Huguenot. Paris erupted in riots and Catherine de Medicini, matriarch of the House of Guise, ordered for the city to be cleansed of Huguenots. A massacre ensued during which more than 10,000 people were murdered. King Philip, Mary Queen of Scots, and the Pope celebrated on hearing the news while Elizabeth wept. Her hands tied by the necessity of maintaining England's alliance with the French, Elizabeth could only offer surreptitious aid to her Protestant allies in France.

In 1574, militant Catholic priests from continental seminaries began to arrive in England with the task of restoring the old faith on English soil. Many of these priests were educated under the patronage of King Philip or the Pope and were rigorously trained for this special undercover mission. Over the next few years, the number of "seminaries" in England rose to over one hundred. Their presence rejuvenated the Catholic faith so much so that the government was forced to act. Thanks to Cecil, now Lord Burghley's, huge network of spies led by Elizabeth's spymaster, Sir Francis Walsingham, a number of priests were arrested, tortured for their knowledge, and subjected to a macabre traitor's death. These executions inspired a cult of martyrdom that attracted many less zealous Catholics to their cause.

In 1575, Henry III of France requested a renewal of the Treaty of Blois and the leaders of the Protestant states of the Netherlands offered Elizabeth the crown for her support of their uprising. As Philip was the hereditary heir and anointed King of the Netherlands, it seemed counterintuitive for Elizabeth to support the deposing of a sovereign and so she declined. During this time of peace Elizabeth made her most famous progress, a grand tour of the homes of the noblest families in the land that culminated in a visit to Kenilworth, where Leicester put on the most extravagant entertainments seen over the course of Elizabeth's entire reign. This legendary visit, which became known as the "princely pleasures," saw Kenilworth Castle transformed into the most extravagant lodgings in all of England save Elizabeth's own, and featured pageants based on Arthurian legend.

After her visit to Kenilworth, Elizabeth and Leicester visited the house of the Earl of Essex, where they were the guest of the Countess Lettice Knollys, who was also Elizabeth's cousin. Before long, Leicester and Lettice were involved in a passionate love affair. Lettice's husband, the Earl of Essex, died of dysentery in September 1576 and, still young and ambitious, Lettice set about making Leicester her husband. Lettice discovered she was pregnant in early 1578 and Leicester agreed to marry her. It was well-known that Leicester was more than ready for married life and desperately wanted a son who could carry on his good name.

It didn't take long for Elizabeth to find out about Leicester's betrayal and she reacted by reopening marriage negotiations with the Duke of Anjou. Leicester removed himself from court for two months, hoping that his absence would encourage Elizabeth's heart to grow fonder. Leicester's approach worked, and Elizabeth begged him never to leave her for so long again. Elizabeth made her position clear: if Leicester could remain loyal to her and behave as though nothing had happened she could too, although she developed an implacable hatred of Lettice and refused to acknowledge her existence ever again. The fact that Leicester was already married when he married Lettice was dealt with strange ease. Leicester had secretly married Douglas Howard in 1573 and had a son with her but managed, with the help of his powerful friends, to have this marriage deemed invalid and his son made illegitimate.

In 1577, Elizabeth had cause to regret her decision not to take the throne of the Netherlands as offered to her by its Protestant leaders in 1575, when the French Duke of Anjou invaded the Netherlands and concluded a treaty that made him their governor. The title "Defender of the Liberties of the Low Countries Against Spanish Tyranny" was a clear provocation to King Philip of Spain. Philip reacted by sending a Spanish army to push William of Orange's forces back into the northern territories. Again, Elizabeth was pressured to take sides and began to consider marrying the Duke of Anjou seriously.

Now forty-five, Elizabeth was concerned that she would be unable to conceive a child and employed a panel of physicians from all over Europe to confirm that she could indeed still conceive. It seemed more likely than ever that the Queen would finally renounce her virgin status and take a husband, and in August the Duke himself made a secret visit to Greenwich to meet the Queen. The visit was brief but significant, as both parties were said to be completely enamored with each other and genuinely excited to be wed.

Yet opposition to the marriage was strong in England, Anjou being both a foreigner and raised Catholic, and even some of Elizabeth's courtiers dared to voice their reservations about it. Elizabeth realized that in order to keep the love of her subjects and to encourage the loyalty and goodwill of her councilors she would have to reject the Duke of Anjou's longstanding proposal and give up her final hope of ever being a wife and mother. This decision proved to be in England's best interests as, in September that year, the Duke accepted the crown of the Netherlands in return for helping Dutch rebels fight against Philip of Spain. Had Elizabeth married the Duke, England could not have avoided being dragged into a long and costly war. As it was the Duke arrived in the Netherlands in February 1582, failed utterly at helping the Dutch Protestant rebels' cause, and eventually turned on the very people he was there to liberate, enraging the Dutch and disgracing his country in the process.

Chapter Eight

Trouble in England

"If these English nobles decide to undertake so glorious a work, they do not commit any sin."

—Pope Gregory XIII

As England entered a new decade, it became isolated once more from the major powers in Europe. In 1580 Pope Gregory XIII reissued the bull against Elizabeth, prompting a resurgence of Catholic resistance in England, helped by the arrival of a new wave of Jesuit missionaries from Rome. Philip of Spain acquired the throne of Portugal, making him the richest and most powerful sovereign in the world, and Mary Queen of Scots made a friend in the Spanish ambassador Mendoza, who encouraged her involvement in a fresh round of plots against Elizabeth.

Although isolated politically, England was now able to exert its influence overseas by entering a period of pioneering geographic exploration. In September 1580, Francis Drake returned to England after a three-year mission to circumnavigate the globe, a feat that had not been repeated since 1522 when Ferdinand Magellan first completed the voyage. During his voyage, Drake had engaged in flagrant piracy with Elizabeth's blessing and had seized over £800,000 of Spanish treasure. Understandably, Philip and his ambassador in England, Mendoza, were enraged and began planning a naval and military attack on England

Not content with reissuing the bull declaring Elizabeth's excommunication, Pope Gregory XIII now made public a pronouncement that sanctioned the assassination of Elizabeth. Asked by two English Catholic lords if it would be illegal to kill Elizabeth, the Pope responded, "If these English nobles decide to undertake so glorious a work, they do not commit any sin." Elizabeth realized that the religious divide in England was a far more dangerous situation than she had supposed and sanctioned a number of far harsher measures against those who attended mass, defamed the Queen, or refused to attend Anglican services.

Yet another plot against Elizabeth was hatched, but this time the Pope, the House of Guise, King Philip of Spain, and Mary Queen of Scots were all involved. The plot became known as Philip's "Enterprise of England" and involved four separate invasions in Ireland, Scotland, Sussex, and Norfolk. Thanks to the work of Elizabeth's spymaster Walsingham, details of the plot filtered through to England, but the threat was very real; Elizabeth again tried to facilitate Mary's return to Scotland without any bloodshed. Elizabeth moved Mary from her comfortable surroundings at Sheffield Castle to the dreary fortress at Tutbury. Despite this, the relationship between Elizabeth and Mary remained amiable, if suspicious, and the pair continued to exchange affectionate letters and gifts. When James VI, Mary's son, betrayed her and refused to agree to Elizabeth's plan to restore Mary to joint ownership of the throne of Scotland, Elizabeth kept it from Mary to spare her feelings.

Elizabeth's security became even more precarious when William of Orange was assassinated in July 1584. The assassination was almost certainly carried out on Philip's orders, and England feared that Elizabeth might be next on his hit list. In 1585, Philip provoked Elizabeth further when he ordered that all English vessels in Spanish-controlled ports be seized and added to his own fleet. In response, Elizabeth made Francis Drake an admiral and sent him on a dangerous voyage to the Caribbean to capture Spain's largest naval bases. With a fleet of 22 ships and over a thousand tough, seafaring men, Drake was successful, and Philip was humiliated. The Dutch were now Elizabeth's only ally, and she quickly signed a treaty with them.

As part of England's treaty with the Dutch, Elizabeth sent an army of 6000 men and 1000 horsemen to protect her Protestant allies against Spanish Catholic aggression. Elizabeth chose Leicester to lead this army as Lieutenant-General, an unusual choice considering Leicester had not engaged in warfare in thirty years, was over fifty years old, and in poor health. Leicester took a household of 170 people with him to the Netherlands including his wife, who insisted on taking a vast amount of luggage and a number of ladies in waiting. Leicester's arrival in the Netherlands gave the Dutch cause for great celebration, and after three weeks of feasting and entertainment, they offered Leicester the position of the Supreme Governor of the Netherlands. Leicester agreed, and when news reached Elizabeth, she exploded with rage, something her courtiers had now grown quite accustomed to witnessing.

That Elizabeth had grown prone to violent tempers and fits of tears was no surprise, considering the pressure she was under. The Netherlands Expedition had been a costly and fruitless affair, and in March of 1586 Philip secured Pope Sixtus V's moral and financial support for his "Enterprise of England," and the invasion took on all of the glorious ideology of a holy crusade. Something had to be done to dissuade Philip from invading England, and soon.

Early in 1586, Walsingham had succeeded in intercepting a young Catholic priest working for Mary Queen of Scots. Although Mary always wrote using a cipher, Walsingham had an expert on hand to decode her letters before re-sealing them and sending them to their final destination. Gifford was forced to tell Mary that he had secured a secret route to smuggle her letters to which Mary reacted with joy and immediately set about making contact with her allies. Through his access to Mary's correspondence, Walsingham was able to learn of a plot to orchestrate a Catholic rebellion at the same time Philip invaded England and in the chaos assassinate Elizabeth.

This plot became known as the Babington plot, as it was a Catholic gentleman by the name of Anthony Babington who volunteered to do the dastardly deed. Babington wrote to Mary directly, outlining his plans, and Walsingham waited with baited breath for Mary's reply.

Around the same time, Mary learned of the Treaty of Berwick, an agreement between Elizabeth and James VI of Scotland that made provision for each monarch to protect the other in the event of an invasion. For Mary, this treaty represented the ultimate betrayal by her only child. Finally, Mary's lengthy reply to Babington's letter arrived and was decoded to reveal that she had offered her full support of his plot to murder Elizabeth. Mary had incriminated herself in the assassination of a sovereign, and Walsingham knew he had to act fast in order to protect Elizabeth and destroy Mary once and for all.

Chapter Nine

Mary's Execution

"I know I have the body but of a weak and feeble woman, but I have the heart and stomach of a king, and of a King of England too, and think foul scorn that Parma or Spain, or any Prince of Europe should dare to invade the borders of my realm."

—Queen Elizabeth I of England

Hearing news that the plot had been uncovered, Babington fled; on 9th of August, 1586 Walsingham rode out to Mary's new home at Chartley, Essex and arrested her personally. The conspirators went to trial and fourteen men in all were condemned to death for their part in the plot. Insisting that the usual execution method for traitors was not nearly punishment enough for the men who had plotted to assassinate her, Elizabeth ordered that the men be disemboweled before being hanged. Once seven of the men had endured this terrible death, Elizabeth relented and ordered that the second set of traitors be hanged until dead and then disemboweled and quartered.

Once the executions took place, the whole of England knew about the plot and Mary's role in it. Pamphlets and ballads circulated and the people were soon baying for the blood of Mary Queen of Scots. Elizabeth abhorred the idea of an anointed Queen being put to death and resisted her councilor's pleas to put Mary on trial for as long as she could. Elizabeth had Mary transferred to Fotheringhay Castle, a Medieval fortress that was far from comfortable but at least spared Mary the trauma of being held in the Tower.

Eventually, Elizabeth capitulated, agreeing that Mary should be tried and appointing thirty-six councilors to act as judges. At first, Mary refused to take part, seeing herself as exempt from England's laws, but Elizabeth wrote to her directly, stating, "You have in various ways and manners attempted to take my life and bring my kingdom to destruction by bloodshed. It is my will that you answer the nobles and peers of the kingdom, as if I were myself present." After a two-day trial, the court found Mary guilty of being an accessory to the conspiracy and of imagining and compassing Her Majesty's destruction, charges punishable by death.

When Parliament assembled on the 29th of October, both the Lords and Commons demanded that Mary be executed. Presented with Parliament's petition, Elizabeth found herself faced with the most difficult decision of her life. Not only was Elizabeth loath to put a fellow female sovereign to death but she was under pressure from Scotland and France to show Mary mercy. At the same time, should she sign the warrant for Mary's execution, England may come under attack from her vengeful Catholic allies.

It is unclear exactly what happened next. Once Elizabeth learned of a plot to liberate Mary from Fotheringhay, she agreed to put Mary to death without delay, signed her death warrant, had it sealed and ordered it to be delivered. Later, Elizabeth said she had changed her mind and ordered that the warrant be held and not delivered. It seems Elizabeth was hoping to shift the responsibility for Mary's death and deny blame by suggesting her orders had not been followed. Elizabeth had even gone so far as to ask one of her councilors to murder Mary in secret so she could announce that she died of natural causes, but no one was willing to commit such an unworthy act.

Mary took the news of her imminent execution incredibly well. She wrote cheerful letters insisting that she was coming to the end of a long pilgrimage and was more than ready to die a martyr's death. Mary wept when she said goodbye to the faithful servants who had served her for decades but composed herself when it was time to walk to the Great Hall at Fotheringhay Castle, where she was to be beheaded. Mary had dressed with great care in a black satin gown and was adorned with a number of crucifixes and a set of prayer beads. When it was time to remove her outer garments so as not to impede the executioner's ax, Mary revealed a bodice and petticoat in scarlet red, the color of Catholic martyrdom. As a Protestant priest recited prayers in English, Mary tried to drown out his voice with her own prayers in Latin and repeated the words "In manuas tuas, Domine, confide spiritum meum" (Into Thy Hands, O Lord, I commend my spirit.) It took two blows to sever Mary's head; once the deed was done a small dog emerged from its hiding place underneath her gowns and lay, shivering, in a pool of her blood.

While England rejoiced, Elizabeth was plunged into despair and immediately regretted signing Mary's death warrant. Elizabeth believed that God would punish her for Mary's execution and for a time she was inconsolable. Neither James VI of Scotland nor Henry III of France tried to punish Elizabeth for Mary's execution, as both believed that their relationship with England was worth preserving, but Catholic Europe reacted to the news with horror, and the Pope called for a new crusade.

As the year 1587 drew to a close England braced herself for war. The Queen appointed Lord Howard, Lieutenant General, Lord High Admiral and Commander of the English Navy and put the country's entire fleet on standby. By the summer of 1588, Elizabeth knew that Philip was ready to attack any day now and had a huge armada of Spanish galleons at his disposal, and yet she still hoped that careful diplomacy might avoid a war.

The Spanish Armada was first sighted by the English on the 19th of July. The English fleet of 150 ships followed the Armada to Calais where Palma, head of the Spanish army, was waiting with 16,000 soldiers to cross the channel. At midnight on the 28th of July, Howard gave the order for a number of fire-ships to be deployed. These flaming ships set a number of the looming Spanish galleons on fire and destroyed the armada's formation giving England the decisive upper hand. Expecting a

Spanish army to arrive on English soil any day, Leicester raised a huge army and equipped them to defend their country. Elizabeth gave a stirring speech in front of hundreds of these troops at Tilbury, Essex dressed in white velvet with a silver breastplate and riding a huge white horse.

Elizabeth cried out, "'I know I have the body but of a weak and feeble woman, but I have the heart and stomach of a king, and of a King of England too, and think foul scorn that Parma or Spain, or any Prince of Europe should dare to invade the borders of my realm."

The defeat of the Spanish Armada was an important victory for England, but it did not bring an end to the war with Spain. The Spanish retained control of the southern part of the Netherlands, and the threat of invasion would hang over England for the rest of Elizabeth's reign. Nonetheless, the people rejoiced, and praise for Elizabeth poured in from all over the world. In France, Rome, and Italy, Catholics praised the strength of the English Queen; in England, Elizabeth's legend grew ever more potent.

Chapter Ten

The Essex Affair

"She certainly is a great Queen, and were she only a Catholic, she would be our greatly beloved daughter. Just look how well she governs! She is only a woman. Only mistress of half an island, and yet she makes herself feared by Spain, by France, by the Empire, by all!"

—Pope Sixtus V

Elizabeth's joy and relief over the outcome of the Spanish invasion were short-lived, as on the 4th of September, 1588, Leicester died, and Elizabeth was stricken with grief. Leicester had been Elizabeth's closest friend for more than thirty years, and his death was a huge blow to the Queen who was forced to behave as though nothing had happened and lead the people of England in their celebrations. Leicester had lived beyond his means and died in debt, something Elizabeth promptly used to punish his widow Lettice by taking back all of Leicester's lands and properties.

Leicester was not the first or the last of Elizabeth's close friends to pass away and leave her. As Elizabeth aged, she was forced to acknowledge that the men who had surrounded her in her youth were dying off and had to be replaced by younger, often more ambitious men.

One such man was Essex, a proud and vain courtier who attracted an aristocratic following at court and had dreams of military valor. Essex became one of Elizabeth's favorites and made Robert Cecil, Lord Burghley's son, his enemy. Another of Elizabeth's favorites was Sir Walter Raleigh, an English gentleman who had fought in France and served as Lord Deputy of Ireland. Handsome and intelligent, Raleigh was quickly added to Elizabeth's posse of favored men and was knighted in 1585. With new arrivals, new factions sprung up in court, and Elizabeth struggled to control this new crowd of courtiers who were increasingly dismissive of the older generation's manners and traditions.

Since the Protestant King Henry IV had inherited the French throne in 1589, he had been begging for military support from the English. Spanish forces were still active in France and helping the French Catholic forces to occupy parts of Brittany and Normandy. The first two English campaigns in France were costly disasters that were completely ineffective in pushing back Spanish troops. In 1591, Elizabeth allowed Essex to head an army with the mission of supporting Henry IV to defeat the Spanish at the besieged city of Rouen. Again the venture was a disaster, and Essex was called back to England, but before he left France, he knighted twenty-four of his supporters without the Queen's consent. To some, this was a petulant act carried out by a man who had grown too bold, but to others, Essex's act was more sinister and represented a clear threat to Elizabeth.

Meanwhile, Raleigh committed a serious offense by secretly marrying and impregnating Bess Throckmorton, one of Elizabeth's maids of honor. It was against the law for those of noble blood to marry without Elizabeth's consent, but as Elizabeth aged she became even more incensed by scandal at court, particularly when it could not be denied that sex had taken place. Elizabeth confined both Raleigh and his bride to the Tower but released Raleigh when a captured Spanish treasure ship was brought into Dartmouth, inciting a riot that only Raleigh could stop.

Despite his terrible performance in France, Elizabeth agreed to appoint Essex as joint commander with Lord Howard on an expedition to destroy Philip's new fleet. Essex was successful in raiding the notoriously rich port of Cadiz but reserved little for the Queen, distributing his loot amongst his men instead. Regardless, the English people loved him and saw him as another Drake, a fearless explorer risking his life on the open seas.

Elizabeth was jealous of Essex's standing with the public and was growing tired of his escalating rudeness that had resulted in a number of very public quarrels. When Burghley died on the 4th of April 1598, Elizabeth took the news badly but had little time to mourn as a major uprising in Ireland had killed over 1200 English soldiers and left English territory in the north undefended. Elizabeth sent Essex to put down the revolt and, yet again, he disappointed her by returning having done more damage than good. In time, it became clear that Essex's misdemeanors were more serious than they appeared. Essex had wasted £300,000 of England's money, deserted during a campaign, and directly disobeyed the Her Majesty's orders. Elizabeth's wrath was terrible, but the public did not share her passion and petitioned for his release from confinement. Elizabeth wanted to have Essex tried for treason but eventually agreed to have him stripped of his titles and ruined financially instead.

In early 1601, Essex plotted to seize control of the government and enlisted a number of willing noblemen to help him. Cecil, Elizabeth's closest advisor now that his father, Burghley, was dead, knew exactly what Essex was planning; when Essex attempted to raise a rebellion on February 8th, 1601 and marched with 100 armed men into the City of London, he was not surprised. Essex raised little support, and when he tried to retreat he was arrested and imprisoned in the Tower of London to await trial. Essex was found guilty of treason and executed in the courtyard of the Tower on the 24th of February 1601, aged 35.

Essex's betrayal had left Elizabeth emotionally bruised and physically weakened. During her long reign Elizabeth had endured much treachery and shown incredible courage in the face of danger but now, aged and alone, she began to break down. A number of Elizabeth's lifelong friends died in 1602 and 1603; Elizabeth grew increasingly depressed, removing herself from court and public life almost completely.

Meanwhile, Cecil had been working diligently behind the scenes to pave the way for King James VI's succession on the event of Elizabeth's death. James requested that

Elizabeth openly acknowledge him as an heir while still on the throne, but if Elizabeth had been touchy about the issue of succession when still a young woman, the subject was positively taboo by now.

In the final years of her reign, Elizabeth presided over a neglected and fatigued court and a famine-stricken England. Struggling to restock her treasury after costly campaigns in Netherland and Ireland, not to mention the cost of keeping a Navy ready to defend against the threat of yet another Spanish Armada, Elizabeth had effectively bankrupted England. In an attempt to reduce the number of citizens dying on the streets, Parliament passed the Poor Act in 1598, which placed the responsibility for caring for destitute people on the local parish.

Elizabeth gave her last speech to Parliament on the 30th of November 1601. This speech became known as the "Golden Speech" and was a bold and proud account of her performance as Queen as well as a loving goodbye to her people.

In March of 1603, Elizabeth became ill with an ulcerated throat, cold symptoms, and fever. Possibly suffering from a strain of influenza, Elizabeth lay on cushions on the floor for days, complaining of a dry mouth and heat in her chest. Elizabeth rapidly developed a severe case of pneumonia, and on the 24th of March 1603, she slipped into a deep sleep from which she never woke.

Conclusion

Just a few hours after Queen Elizabeth I's death, the accession of King James VI of Scotland, Mary Queen of Scots' only child, to King James I of England was proclaimed at Whitehall. Five days after Elizabeth's death, her body was prepared for her coffin by her ladies in waiting. Her coffin was then taken downriver to Whitehall on a barge lit with torches where it lay in state for a number of days. On the 28th of April, thousands lined the route of from Whitehall to Westminster Abbey to watch Elizabeth's funeral procession. A hearse, drawn by four horses, hung with black velvet and topped with a life-sized wax effigy of the queen, took Elizabeth's body to her final resting place at Westminster Abbey where she shared a tomb with her sister, Mary Tudor. James I funded a magnificent tomb for Elizabeth that was completed in 1606.

Elizabeth had given her people the gift of a stable government and relative peace for the forty-five years of her reign. The England Elizabeth inherited was an impoverished island nation; although she died in unavoidable debt, she had overseen England's magnificent rise to one of the greatest and most feared nations in Europe. Elizabeth gained the epithet "The Queen of the Sea" thanks to the success of her Navy and how she artfully avoided full-scale religious war in a country that was deeply divided along religious lines.

In her famous Golden Speech, Elizabeth said,

"Mr. Speaker, we perceive your coming it to present thanks unto us. Know that I accept them with no less joy than your loves can have desired to offer at such a present. I do assure you, there is no prince that loves his subjects better. There is no jewel, be it of never so rich a price, which I set before this jewel: I mean your love. For I do more esteem it than any treasure or riches, for those we know how to prize: but loyalty, love and thanks – I account them invaluable: and though God hath raised me high, yet this I account the glory of my crown, that I have reigned with your loves. This makes me that I do not so much rejoice that God hath made me to be a queen, as to be a queen over so thankful a people and to be the means under God to conserve you in safety and to preserve you from danger."

Under the rule of King James I, the English people came to realize what had set Elizabeth apart from other monarchs and there was a resurgence of respect for the memory of the Virgin Queen.

Made in the USA
San Bernardino, CA
21 February 2018